Getting
and
Staying
CLEAN

Getting and Staying CLEAN

DOUGLAS K. CAIN JR.

Xulon Press

Xulon Press
2301 Lucien Way #415
Maitland, FL 32751
407.339.4217
www.xulonpress.com

© 2017 by Douglas K. Cain JR.

All rights reserved solely by the author. The author guarantees all contents are original and do not infringe upon the legal rights of any other person or work. No part of this book may be reproduced in any form without the permission of the author. The views expressed in this book are not necessarily those of the publisher.

Unless otherwise indicated, Scripture quotations taken from the King James Version (KJV) – *public domain.*

Printed in the United States of America.

ISBN-13: 978-1-54561-228-6

Contents

Acknowledgment vii

Introduction ix

Admitting You Have a Problem 1

Take Responsibility for Your Actions 6

Seek God Even More 14

Leave people and places Alone 20

Your Healing Begins. 25

Acknowledgment

First, I would like to give thanks and honor to God my Father, for never leaving nor forsaking me and for hearing my cry for help. To my wife, Idella: for accepting me for who I was and helping me to become who I am today. If only you knew how much you helped me to grow spiritually and help guiding me to become a true husband. I will always love and support you dear.

To my kids, Lil-Doug, Shateya, Douquonna, DaQuan, Dou'Yonna and Dre'Shaun: Thanks for your continued love and support when you didn't understand why I had to leave our hometown. You kids mean the world to me, I will always love you guys.

To my stepsons Aaron, Thadius, and Dionte: You young men did something most young men would not do, you guys hung in there with me and my mess and allowed me to be apart you and your mom lives. Again thanks for seeing the good in me also for accepting me in your lives even though I made it hard at times. Thanks for hanging in there .Love you guy's.

To my brother-in-law, Jerome: thanks for all the spiritual counseling and brotherly talks; you are truly one big brother.

Finally, the biggest thanks goes out to the woman who carried me for nine months. Thank you, Mother Linda, for raising a little boy into a man. I know it wasn't easy; yet, after all I put you through and some of the disrespect I should you your love for me never faded. My love for you will never fade either. Much love and thanks for being my mom. I love you mom, you are the greatest!

Introduction

I was inspired to write this book on the behalf of my past experience with drugs and alcohol, mostly to tell the world how God brought me out of my troubled times.

To all the men, women, boys, and girls that have an addiction to drugs, alcohol, or both: I want to tell you that there is a way out that doesn't cost a dime—just your time and belief in our creator Himself, God.

After twenty-five years of drug use and thirty years of alcoholism, I can say you don't have to go to jail or a treatment center. If you are tired of the life > you are living and have no money, read this entire book and start a new relationship with self, Christ, and life.

Admitting you Have a Problem

There are five stages that you must process in your life in order for you to get and stay clean of all drugs and alcohol. The first stage is the most important stage of all. Without this first stage, you will never get nor stay clean. It's important that you see, recognize, and admit there is a problem with the use of drugs and alcohol. Without this being done, there isn't anything or anyone that can help you—not even God. I'm here to tell you if this first stage doesn't take place, don't waste your time or anyone else's time because you are not ready. I can surely say you are doomed from the start if this doesn't take place. God won't even help you if you are not ready. He will help those that help themselves. I say this because when [You] notice or acknowledge that your use of drugs or alcohol are hindering you from moving forward in life, it shows a desire deep down in the soul is crying out for help.

When you cry out from your soul, it comes from the heart and God hears those types of cries. Again, He only helps those that want to be helped. Neither I nor anyone else can cry out for you; it must come from your own heart. Family and friends can tell you all day that you need help; you go get it and it won't last long. You will surely relapse if you get clean for others. I know you are thinking, what is this person talking about? They must have lost their mind. Let me share this with you: the fact is, when you try to get clean for others, you put all your energy and efforts into pleasing them and not yourself. The first time the ones you are doing this for show you grief or say something you don't like, and you've only been clean for, let's say, four months, you start thinking, What am I doing this for? They're still not happy. Here's another thought: This is the thanks I get for trying. See the problem is you want appreciation from them and for them; it hasn't been long enough for them to trust or believe in you yet. The problem is because you did this for them, so you don't yet understand why they feel this way still and for this let down, at least in your mind, you start to say, "What am I doing this for?" Here is where you start feeling worthless again. Once this thought enters your mind, relapse has gained control of you and your mind.

Guess what happens next? You will, I say you will, find away to get high and/or drunk again. Failure has again taken over you. To prevent this from happening, get clean for yourself and not others. When you notice that you yourself have a problem, right then at that point in time, you don't even realize it but you now want help. What has started to happen to you is deep within you, your soul has gotten tired of the damage you have caused it. At this point in your life, you have gotten tired of yourself and want a better life for you. Now it's about you and what you want for you. That's why I say you must admit it to yourself because then and only then will you realize your life does have meaning.

Now you will begin to show yourself first as well as others that you want to change your life for the better. This way, you will only look for a pat on the back from yourself. One of my favorite sayings is, "I can't love anyone else until I first love me." Since you have a mind now to make a change in your life, all things that have hindered you in life are about to stop and come to a head. What I'm saying is, all the pain and agony that you put your body through is about to surface. The good part of this is that because you have recognized your problem and doing something about it, you have started the process of something beautiful.

I want to warn you, though, because of the decision you have chosen to make in your life, it's going to get a bit rough. The reason for this act is that, you once was working and living for—the devil and he was fine. Now that your mind and heart have been changed, he is mad and angry with you. Here's what you need to do: keep the vision of the reason you decided to make the change in your life in the first place alway's in the back of your mind. It will be crucial to your recovery. Write down the date that you cried out for help and felt the need for change in your life. Keep this date in your mind at all times. This date will be a shield for you and protection from the devil. With this you will always have some kind of power over the devil to work with. It will always help you when you remember the day when you saw something in yourself that you didn't like that made you want to change. The devil is going to come at you from all sorts of directions because he doesn't want to loose you. You must remember when your soul cried out, God heard you and so did the devil. Keep crying out every time you feel pressure. God will keep you from the devil's grasp. So today, if you are reading this book, love yourself, and finally have or want to admit your addiction, continue to read and see how wonderful your life can be drug and alcohol free.

Take Responsibility for Your Actions

Here is where it gets a little tricky, yet this was the easiest of the processes for me at least. Once you admit your addictions, God will start opening your eyes to your past and what your future can be. For years, while going through your addiction stages of your life, you blamed everyone for your troubled times, like you was mister-goody-two-shoes. No matter what the situation may have been, you would always put the blame on others. It was always, for example, "They made me do it. If they had only left me alone. I had a rough childhood." Or, my favorite: "No one loves me." Let's just take a moment, sit back, take a deep breath and relax. Now think back to the very first time you took your first drink or tried drugs for the first time. That's right: no one made you do it, did they? No, you may have been cheered on or curious or wanted to fit in or seem cool. The point is [You] could have said, "No," yet you didn't; the choice was yours. You alone made a conscious decision to use or drink what you did. A lot of times in our lives, we make the wrong decision because we at that time in our life didn't know Christ Jesus. The first time you tired anything, it seemed to be the thing to do—at least, it felt like it at that point in time in your life. After a while, life with drugs and alcohol feels like it is the thing to do. The drugs and alcohol had started to control your mind and body. The more you did, the more corrupted you became. Your life started going downhill. This is when you start blaming others—even the ones you get high and drink with. All the wrongdoings in your life are your fault. Hear me clearly: in order to recover completely you must know this, receive this, and lastly, accept it. The problems in your life is because of your life decisions not no ones else. The fact of the matter is that you need to understand and realize that you hurt you and when this happens you will start to feel different also start seeing > clearly what you need to do for you. It's okay to look at you and tell you that you are sorry for the hurt you caused you; a sense of relief should overflow you at that moment. I say all of this to you to say that when I came to the recognition that I had a problem and I was my problem there will have to be a lot of work to be put in on staying clean. God started opening up my eyes. I started seeing all those that I had hurt, along with the true hurt and damage that I caused to myself. At that point in my life, I wanted to make right all my wrongs. I just didn't know how to let stuff go; I was in a bad relationship and my pastor at that time told me it was going to get better, but it didn't. People prophesied that everything would work out all right and that God was with the relationship; nothing changed. I knew something wasn't right and that I needed more powerful help so I start to read my bible more and more so I got closer to God than man and things start to change. There were voices in my head telling me to leave, but I thought it was the devil; then one day, I cried out to God for help and He assured me that it was his voice that I heard. Even after the voice of God spoke to me, I still struggled because I believe more of what the pastor and people prophesying to me said because I didn't believe I was worthy enough to hear from God myself, but because God loves me, He continued to speak to me more and more the more of my time I gave God the more He spoke to me. It wasn't until then that He made me understand that I was worthy of hearing from Him for myself. God has a way of dealing with us all in different ways, but with the same results. The only way we can take on our responsibilities, whatever they may be (good or bad) is to cry out to God from our heart. When it comes from the heart, its true, it's real, it's love, and it's of God.

I can remember it like it was yesterday when I first reached this point in my life. I was incarcerated and the Lord spoke to me and told me to write letter to all those that I had hurt. It wasn't easy because I was

locked up for something I didn't do, so I questioned God. I was mad with God. Then the Lord spoke to me again and said, "Remember all the wrong you did do and I kept you?" Not knowing at the time God allowed me to be sent to jail because of the life I was living and He needed to get my attention. He knew He wasn't going to get it as long as I was on the streets. When I finally saw what God was doing, I sat on my bunk in my cell and cried because God was right.

Later that night, as I slept the Lord showed me that He wanted to use me and this was His way of getting my attention. The next morning, I started writing those letters. The first one was to my mother apologizing for all the hurt and disrespect I caused and showed her. Believe me, as I wrote the letter to my mom, I cried like a little baby. I hurted so badly because of the hurt I caused to the woman that gave me life and raised me without a father. How could I hurt her? After mom's letter, I wrote about ten more letters.

When all the letters were done and sent off, about a week later, God started using me. The first way was in the jail choir, then the school as a math tutor for other inmates to prepare them for their G.E.D. I went on to minister to other guys on my tier. They started calling me "preacher man." None of this would have taken place if I hadn't let the first two processes take place from within my heart.

God will only help us when we are real with Him. He knows a fake cry and through Him is the only way. When you take on your responsibility and ask for forgiveness and mean it, you not only reach God, you also reach people because it comes from the heart. Let me tell you this: God may not use you in the same manner as He did me, but He does want to use you if you let Him. There may come a time when you may feel like giving up—please don't. Here's why you may feel this way. Let's say it's been about ten months now and you have been doing all that you have been told to do by the Word of God, your pastor, and others in general. According to you, you don't think you have gotten all that you think you should have gotten by now. Not from God or anyone. You have heard the preacher preach, "Do right by God" and "the Bible says He will never leave you nor forsake you. He will not only give you what you need, but He will give you the desires of your heart." This is true; what he/she reluctantly didn't explain to you is that there are two things you must understand.

The first is yes, God is always with us, but He makes us do nothing. If He gave us all that we want at once, we wouldn't call on or need Him again until we were without again. That would be using God and He won't let that happen. Secondly, who are we to rush God? For example, let's use me. I used drugs and alcohol for over thirty years. For most of my life, I served the devil and God watched and waited on me through all my unfaithfulness, yet He still kept me. Here's the big question I ask you: how long have you been doing wrong and are still here? Is it right for you to turn your back on your creator who kept you? You tell me you can't wait for God to clean you up inside and out it's going to take some time you have put your body through some stuff so let God do what he can do for you without you rushing him. So don't leave Him when things don't seem right to you . I refuse to turn away from Him. When I was incarcerated, He kept me after rehab and relapsing; He kept me while I tried to hang myself—He broke the rope. Doing all of the above, I still left the hand of God. I started getting high again, drinking again, and lost everything He had given me. Sometimes, God will give us what we ask for, knowing we're not ready for it, to let us no hey you really wasn't ready for this. I was one who got what I asked for and left him. I struggled for many years to get it back, but waited because He waited on me. Some don't get that second chance; so I'm asking you once God extends His hand to you, don't let it go. It's by God's grace that I'm still here. I was like the walking dead when I left God. I've seen a lot of people go away from here lost. Don't be lost, please. On July 15, 2012, I sat in my truck at a park crying to God like never before. I was scared and felt death on me. I had never been scared in my life. I asked God to forgive me for all the wrong I've done and for not being pleasing unto His eyes. I asked him to help me. My exact words were, "Lord, I know I go to church, try to do right, know right from wrong, and yet I still do continue to do wrong. How, Lord, do I stop? Show me, God so that I may live right." He heard my cry from my heart; He felt my pain and gave me another chance. My advice to you would be never leave the one that created you and blew the breath of life in you. When God gives you a chance to make your life right, take hold of it and don't let go. Neither of us know the day nor time that we are going to leave this earth, so change now. It's never too late to change as long as you have breath in your body, but when you are gone from this earth, it's too late.

Seek God Even More

If you have reached this part of the process, blessings to you: there is a promise on your life. At this point you have to show your strength in faith and willingness to stay clean. You will need to start focusing even harder on the path in life that you want. Seeking God is where your protection from the enemy truly comes from. Let me explain to you what has taken place, starting with the first process. God gave you some help to see who you had become. Your spirit cried out for help. He heard your soul cry out and opened your eyes. It's like this: there's a gift in you that the Lord wants to use, so He gave you a boost. Everyone doesn't have this type of gift. People that go through something in life that bare these special gifts. Not everyone gets the chance to let God show him or her these special gifts. If you don't believe me, read the Bible. All the people that God used went through something or were born with something, so, you are special. That's why you must seek God so that you can give birth to your special gift. The Bible says many are called but only few are chosen (Matthew 22:14). In the second process of this, God showed you what you needed to do to be at peace with yourself and with others. Now you must seek Him for yourself even more to show Him your faith and love for Him. I'm not saying He will leave you because He won't. What I'm saying is that the longer it takes you to put all your trust in Him the longer it's going to take you to properly heal. I must warn you: we as humans find it hard to seek God when things don't seem to be going our way or may I say taking to long in our eye's.

Here's why: when we get introduced to Christ, the first thing we think is that life is going to be without problems. Wrong! There are sixty-six books in the Bible and none of them speaks of this. It does say in Matthew 11:30: "for my yoke is easy and my burden is light." Hebrews 13:5 says, "I will never leave you nor forsake thee." Proverbs 8:17 says, "I love them that love me: and those that seek me early shall find me. Here in the book of Matthew God is telling us that we can come to Him when time get to troubling and he will make it easy for us but we in return must trust and believe in Him. God has never left anyone, whether we be good or bad yet we always leave

Him, He just there waiting for us to give in and call on Him." You must seek Him morning, evening, and night to stay strong. A lot of people are not going to like who you are starting to become, including family. It will be okay; keep praying for them and yourself. The devil heard you when you finally told yourself that you had a problem; he also saw you take on your responsibility. At this point, he wasn't too worried. When he saw you sought God's help, he panicked and got angry. Now that he knows you truly want to clean up your life, he will do anything to keep you, even kill you. He's angry because he is loosing a good worker. I know; why do I say this? Think about when you were bad. You were good at it, weren't you? Yes, you were. Now that you have chosen to take the right track in life, switch it around and be a great worker or mighty ambassador for God. The more you progress in the work, further down the road and only then will it get easier to hurdle the obstacles that will appear before sent by satan himself. Be careful because the devil is tricky and will use anything and everything to try to mess your life up again. I can remember when I came home from being incarcerated and stayed with my mother. All was well for about five months. Then the devil stepped in and caused havoc between mom and me.

Mom start getting on me about coming in the house too late, so her doors could be locked by 10:00p.m. That didn't set well with me. Here I was, a grown man, and she telling me to be in by ten o'clock. Even though I was mad, I did as she wished because it was her house. After that, we started having all kinds of problems with each other. I found a job, and after working for about four months, I moved out of my mom's house. All was good, but I still carried that anger for my mom. That anger lead me to question God and I got back on drugs and alcohol. This took place back in 2006 when I got out of jail fresh on the streets and got weak in the flesh. I pray this book prevent you from making the same mistake. Don't allow or let anyone get you away from God. When I left my mom's house with that anger, it was one of the biggest mistakes of my life. I stopped seeking God and lost everything, including my mind. It's by God's grace and mercy that I'm still here today. So I'm asking you to not give up on God; there's no job too big for Him.

So give your life totally to Him, pray for everything, and don't hold on to anger, or it will destroy you. Don't do as I did and lose your will to stay strong; stand tall and keep your faith. It will take so much to get it all back. So many major changes are going to start to take place in your life, so find a church to attend; make sure you do this; it's important. Also, set an appointment to see the pastor and share your story about your addiction with him so that you can get the proper guidance you will need. Start a praying life to build a personal relationship with God. He will honor that. Also, find a free clinic in your state that will help you with medication if needed. Trust me; you won't stay on them forever if you stay with God. He will deliver you from them. Just remember that just because you accept Christ, other problems in your life don't stop. God just makes them easier to deal with and He can wipe them away just like he will do with your additions, if you let Him.

[Seek God Seek God Seek God Seek God]

When no one else is there, God will be there anytime, day or night. He will never criticize you when you make a mistake. He will love you when you think you don't deserve it and will lift you up when you fall. If you just keep the faith, believe in Him, and call on Him, He will keep you clean if you allow Him. So do as Matthew 6:33 says, "Seek first the kingdom of God and his righteousness, and all these things shall be added to you." If you seek Him and keep Him in your heart, He will wipe away your past and make your future clear. Don't forget to keep praying morning, noon, and night to build a personal relationship with God; He will honor it. God wants to be first in our lives.

Leave People and Places Alone

This is the biggest problem of all to me, and the hardest to accomplish. The first part of this is leaving the people you dealt with previously. You must stop hanging with all the folks that you got high or drunk with and believe me: it's not easy as it sounds. I just didn't know how to let stuff or people go. The reason is you/me start to think that we have built a relationship with those people. Here's an example, I was in a bad relationship; my pastor told me it would get better, but it didn't. People prophesied that everything would work out and that God was with the relationship, but nothing changed. I stayed in this relationship until we started to hate one another just because I trusted the word of others. There was a voice in my head telling me to get out of the relationship, but I thought it was the devil speaking to me. Then, one day, I cried out to God and asked for His help and He said to me that it is His voice that I am hearing. That was the voice of God telling me to get out and to leave the situation that I was in and that things will start to get better. I left and my life slowly started to work in my favor. You must trust that gut feeling you get in the inside of you when things just don't seem right, it's the spirit of God speaking to you to get out, leave and to avoid the situation. I've talked with at least one hundred or more ex-addicts and all of them said the same thing: letting go of their friends was hard to do. This was a difficult situation for me to process because deep down inside, I truly thought these people were my friends. You know I only thought like this because of the drug and alcohol use. Let me say this: they were never truly your friends. In reality, they were only there for the drugs. Think back when the drugs were gone. So were they, am I right? They didn't care for you. Don't believe me? Try telling them that you are starting and wanting to clean up your life. Now watch their response. They will start saying stuff like, "Maybe someday, not now". Better yet, they may laugh in your face and say, "Hey, I know someone with some good stuff. Let's go get some. We can talk about this later some other day." Don't feel bad; I had to go through this period also. If you think about it, they were just "get high buddies." Instead of them saying, "You can do it" or, "Let's do it together," like a real friend would have done, they just keep trying to feed it to you. The reason why they act like this other than not being your true friend is that they may have heard this from you before. It wasn't until I put it in my mind and heart to quit and change associates that my life started to change for the better. You have to be careful of the people you hang around now; if not, you will get caught up in doing the wrong things again. You must find a batch of friends that want the same godly things that the new you now want out of life.

The second part of this process is that you must stop going to the places where you hung out. It only will be failure for you if you go back there. It takes a while before you can be around those old spots and people again. When you do, it should only be in passing; speaking and keep on moving. If not, this is what I call the entrapment phase. This is where, after a while of being clean, we think we got it made and can go visit old people and spots again. You think you can hang out and be fine—you're wrong. I'm here to tell you: you will fall victim to relapse if you try this. The truth is that you will never be able to hang out at those old spots and people again. I myself fail this process so many times because I failed to continue to seek God like I should have.

Without Him you will too. When you're getting high or drunk, your mind shifts to dumb mode, and you just don't think straight. After doing this for so long, you began to think the people you are around are truly your best friends and the things you all do are so grand. I thought the people I hung around were all the friends I had in the world, so I wasn't letting them go. As time moved on and I worked harder on staying clean from my addictions, I started to see people and places for what they truly were and that they meant me no good. Believe me when I say I got so high and drunk that I didn't know how I would get better. Here I am today, three years clean of drugs and alcohol, and as happy as I've ever been in my life. God has given me a loving wife. I'm well respected in my community and church. My stepsons accept and respect me. My kids may not understand right now why their dad left home but they stilll love and support me. Yes I didn't only leave my home I left my home state, I battered with God on this I didn't want to leave my kid's. God assured me that if I do His will that He will take care of my kids. I say all this to say what ever God ask of you don't be afraid to do it. At this point of my life, I have all I need and most of all I'm free in body, mind, and soul.

It's all because I had a made up my mind to get free from my addictions and stuck with it this time around. Remember this: God only help those who help themselves.

YOUR HEALING BEGANS

I want to start off here with the healing process by stating how blessed I am to be able to express the greatfulness in my heart to be able to share this part of my life with those that read this book. The healing process is an amazing part of getting and staying clean at least for me. It had me worried at times but God picked me by showing his amazing power.

What has happened to you and I was that from the first day you and I choice the addiction of our choice and started to become someone we wasn't. Everyday after that we became an evil creature and for me some of my family did not want to be around. At times I didn't realize the person I had become, then that day came when I was tired of that evil person I saw in myself and decided that I wanted to change. I cried out, God heard me and answered me. God game me inventory of my life and allowed me to see all the damage that I caused my organs inside me. This was scary for me at times. Yes, I got to feeling down but he assured me that my body can be healed if I just believe in him. All this sounds good, don't it? I know it does because it did to me. Let me tell you this, it's a process to it. There is work for you in it. God knows that no addict ever woke up and asked to be one. It's just a trial in some of our lives that we have to go through. In any healing to take place in our lives we must give it to him, then put in the work. What is the work? First, we must call on his great name and believe he can heal us.

Here's how I allowed God to help me. I was staying dizzy and felt faint, everyday, I just took aspirin, thought I was having withdrawals from not using. I passed out at church one day and was rushed to the hospital and found out I had bleeding ulcers. I lost so much blood that I could have died because I didn't like going to the hospital I didn't know what was going on inside of me. God saved me because I chose him. What I'm saying is God put resources out here for us to use them, that's how we help him help us. So find a doctor to go to, take your medication that is prescribed for you, if you want a job go put in applications, the job is not coming to you. Whatever you need to do, go do it. Now, I go to the doctor like I should, take my medication like I should and guess what, those bleeding ulcers I had are gone, look at God. It's never to late for God to heal you. First and most importantly, your mind will start to heal. Yes, your mind is the most important part of the healing and not the heart. Most people do think it's the heart. During my experience I've found it to be true that the mind leads the body. There had been times in my life that I felt a way about a situation, went with it and it was the wrong thing to do. The mind is a thought mechanism that feeds the heart which is a feeling mechanism. Your mind must first process or think the situation through, send it down to the heart, where the heart feels the situation out. Then the heart send it back to the mind that now have a plan with the feeling that can make the right decision. Then and only then can you body start healing from all the damage you have caused it. this process can be lengthy depending on how long you have been using.

For your healing to be complete you must not let nothing separate you from God. You have to have him deep, I mean deep down in your mind and soul.

I pray that this book help you with the start you will need to lead a better and clean life free of "Drugs and Alcohol. Blessings to you on your new and better journey in your life.

Sincerely, Douglas K. Cain Jr

www.ingramcontent.com/pod-product-compliance
Lightning Source LLC
LaVergne TN
LVHW021744060526
838200LV00052B/3456